Cambridge **Discovery Education**™
▶ **INTERACTIVE READERS**

Series editor: Bob Hastings

THE SCIENCE OF LIGHT

A2⁺

Kathryn O'Dell

CAMBRIDGE UNIVERSITY PRESS
Cambridge, New York, Melbourne, Madrid, Cape Town,
Singapore, São Paulo, Delhi, Mexico City

Cambridge University Press
32 Avenue of the Americas, New York, NY 10013-2473, USA

www.cambridge.org
Information on this title: www.cambridge.org/9781107681989

First published 2014

Printed in Hong Kong, China, by Golden Cup Printing Company Limited

A catalog record for this publication is available from the British Library.

Library of Congress Cataloging-in-Publication Data

O'Dell, Kathryn.
 The science of light / Kathryn O'Dell.
    pages cm. -- (Cambridge discovery interactive readers)
  ISBN 978-1-107-68198-9 (pbk. : alk. paper)
  1. Light--Juvenile literature. 2. English language--Textbooks for foreign speakers. 3. Readers
(Elementary) I. Title.

QC360.O44 2013
535--dc23

                              2013016898

ISBN 978-1-107-68198-9

Additional resources for this publication at www.cambridge.org

Layout services, art direction, book design, and photo research: Q2ABillSMITH GROUP
Editorial services: Hyphen S.A.
Audio production: CityVox, New York
Video production: Q2ABillSMITH GROUP

Contents

Before You Read: Get Ready! 4

CHAPTER 1
See the Light 6

CHAPTER 2
Night Light 8

CHAPTER 3
Natural Light 12

CHAPTER 4
Artificial Light 18

CHAPTER 5
What Do You Think? 24

After You Read 26

Answer Key 28

Glossary

Before You Read: Get Ready!

Light is all around us – in sunlight, stars, and electric lamps – and there are many ways we use light in our lives.

Words to Know

Read the paragraph. Then complete the sentences with the correct highlighted words.

Cosmologists are scientists who study the stars and planets in the universe. They also study the sun, the star that gives light and energy to our planet, Earth.

1 _____ are worlds that move around suns.

2 _____ are people who study things in the sky.

3 The _____ is everything in space.

4 We get _____ from the sun, gas, or oil.

? APPLY

What are some ways that we use energy on Earth?

Words to Know

Read the definitions. Then complete the sentences with the correct form of the highlighted words.

artificial light: light made by people, such as a light bulb and laser light

laser: a very strong line of light that people use for many things, for example to help repair parts of the body

reflect: when light hits something and then changes direction

shine: make bright light

wave: the way some types of energy, like light, move

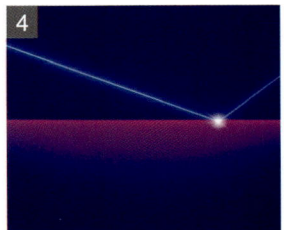

1. The sun _____ through a window.
2. The light from the sun _____ off the water.
3. _____ helps us to do many things, like see at night.
4. The company uses different _____ to help repair computers.
5. Our boat was hit by a large _____ in the ocean.

CHAPTER 1

See the Light

WHAT IS LIGHT?

Lucy stayed up late one night. She slept through her alarm the next morning. Her father came into her bedroom. He turned on the light and shouted, "Get up now, Lucy. It's late!"

Lucy answered, "Dad, the light's shining in my eyes. It hurts! Please turn it off."

Her father didn't listen to her, "You're going to be late for school! Why are you still in bed?"

"Dad," she explained, "I had to work after school. Then I stayed up late studying because I have a test today."

Lucy's explanation brought the problem to light. Now her father understood why she was so tired. He felt bad. His daughter was the light of his life, and he didn't like to fight with her. "Oh," he said, "I'm sorry I was so angry. Let's get you to school."

"I know. I can't miss my test!" Lucy said. She looked worried.

Her father said, "I know you're working hard. But don't worry, there's a light at the end of the tunnel.[1]"

Lucy asked, "What do you mean?"

"You know, things seem bad right now, but you'll soon be on vacation," her father answered.

Lucy said, "Yeah, but right now that feels like light years away!"

"It will be here before you know it," her father said, "Now, I give you the green light to sleep as late as you want on Saturday!"

Lucy laughed. "Thanks, Dad."

The word "light" is used in many expressions.[2] Most of them are about things getting better or looking brighter. This may be because light helps us see, and we couldn't live without it. But what is light exactly?

[1]**tunnel:** a long, covered road under earth or through a mountain
[2]**expression:** a group of words that have a special meaning

? UNDERSTAND

Look at the expressions that use "light" on pages 6 and 7. Can you explain what they mean? Try to use them in other sentences.

This is what some cosmologists think the Big Bang looked like.

CHAPTER 2

Night Light

IS THERE LIGHT IN SPACE?

Have you ever looked at the stars and thought about light? Cosmologists try to answer questions about stars, planets, and other things in space. They think the universe started about 14 billion years ago. They believe that all the matter[3] in the universe was in a small ball. This ball got very hot and **expanded** really quickly. They call this the Big Bang Theory. Cosmologists believe that a lot of **energy** came out of the Big Bang. It **spread** matter out across the universe. This matter became cooler, and after millions of years, stars and planets were created. As the universe expanded and cooled, matter lost energy and some became light. Cosmologists are still learning more about this oldest light in the universe.

[3]**matter:** everything in the universe

The sun's light gives us seasons.

Cosmologists know that light comes from stars. The light on the Earth comes from one star, the sun. The Earth turns as it travels around

The Earth gets light from the sun.

the sun. This movement gives us day and night. When a place on the Earth is facing the sun, it is daytime there. When it is turned away from the sun, it is nighttime.

The sun's light also gives us seasons. The Earth takes one year to go round the sun. But the Earth is tilted.[4] So when it travels around the sun, it is summer in the part that is closer to the sun and it is winter in the part that is tilted away.

Often the moon looks really bright, but it doesn't make its own light. It **reflects** light from the sun. The sun's light shines on different parts of the moon as the moon travels around the Earth. That is why the moon looks different at different times of the month.

[4]**tilt:** have one side higher than the other

The sun isn't the only star in the sky, but it's the only one we see during the day. We can see about 2,500 stars in the night sky, but there are many more stars in space.

Long ago, people looked at groups of stars and saw pictures. They created stories, called myths,[5] about these pictures. For example, people saw two bears in the stars, so they created myths about how the bears got there.

Today, we know that stars are made of gases that give off light and heat. Cosmologists can't see all the stars in the universe, but they can see many of them with large **telescopes**. Now we know there are billions and billions of stars in the universe!

[5] **myth:** an old story that explains an event in the natural world

Stars are all different sizes. The sun looks small from the Earth, but it is actually huge – it is bigger than one million Earths!

Stars are also different colors, too. Hot stars look white or blue. Cooler stars look red or orange. Our sun may feel hot to us, but compared to other stars, it is nice and cool.

The Hubble telescope

Stars can be many different colors.

Cosmologists use telescopes to learn about the stars. The Hubble telescope is special because it is in space. It can see farther than telescopes on Earth. By using the Hubble telescope, cosmologists learned about a star cluster[6] called NGC 6397. The stars in this cluster are so close together that two of them sometimes hit each other. When two stars hit each other, they become one star that is very bright.

[6]**cluster:** a group of things close to each other that are like each other

Video Quest

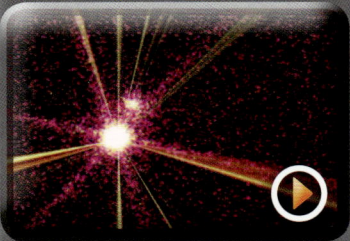

Light Years

Watch this video to find out how far the moon is from the sun and from Earth. How far away are the stars Proxima Centauri and Sirius?

CHAPTER 3

Natural Light

WHAT DOES LIGHT DO FOR US?

People, plants, and animals need sunlight. They cannot live without it. Sunlight helps things live and grow. But it also gives us the colors that we see.

Light waves have seven colors: red, orange, yellow, green, blue, indigo, and violet. When light hits something, some of the light waves are reflected, and some are absorbed.[7]

People only see the colors that are reflected. For example, when light hits a tomato, the orange, yellow, green, blue, indigo, and violet waves are absorbed. The red waves are reflected, so the tomato looks red. If something reflects all of the light waves, it looks white. If it absorbs all of the waves, it looks black.

[7]**absorb:** take in something and hold it

Sunlight helps people in many ways. For example, sunlight helps the body make vitamin D.[8] Vitamin D is needed for strong teeth and bones.[9]

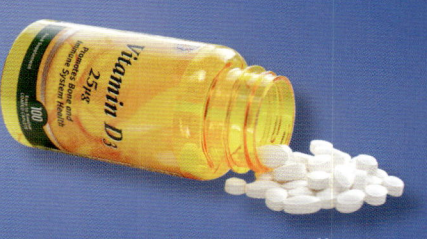

Vitamin D pills

In some parts of the world, people don't get enough sun. For example, in northern countries like Canada and Norway, people often don't get much natural sunlight in the winter. One doctor said that 80 percent of her patients do not get enough vitamin D. This is called vitamin D deficiency. People with vitamin D deficiency need to eat foods with vitamin D or take vitamin D pills. If not, they can have problems with their health.

[8]**vitamin D:** a natural thing that your body needs to be healthy, found in food like eggs and fish

[9]**bones:** the hard, white parts inside our bodies

It's important to get some sun, but not too much. If you spend too long in strong sunlight, you can get a sunburn. Your body sends blood to the burned skin to try and repair it. This is why burned skin looks red.

People with darker skin can take more sun than people with lighter skin. However, anyone can get a sunburn. Doctors say we should use sunblock if we plan to be in the sun a long time. Sunblock stops the sun's energy from burning the skin.

Sun can hurt the body in other ways. For example, too much sun over time can make the skin very dry. It hurts the outside part of the skin, which can make skin look older and give people wrinkles.[10]

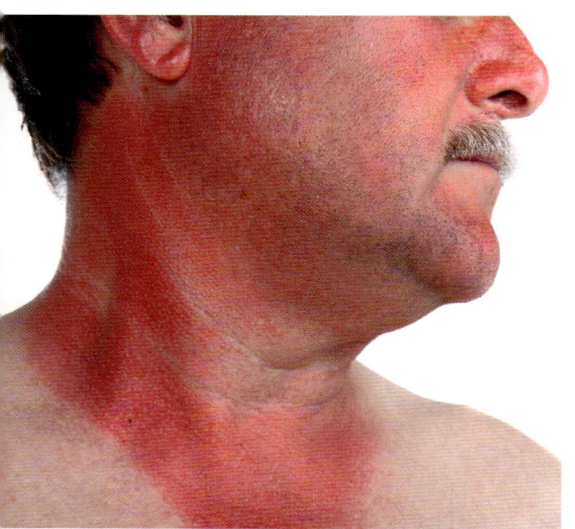

A sunburn on a person's skin

....
[10]**wrinkles:** small lines on your face that you get when you grow old

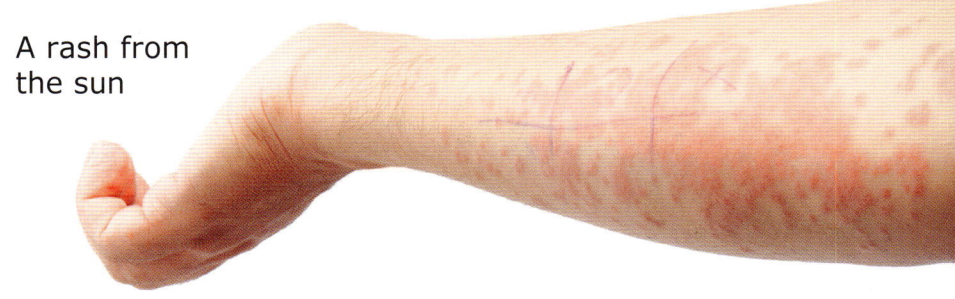
A rash from the sun

Some people are allergic[11] to the sun. They get rashes on their arms and legs when they spend time in the sun. People who are allergic to the sun often cover their bodies even in hot weather. They need to stay out of the sun as much as possible.

In places that are very far north, like Alaska, people have to live without much sunlight all winter. But in summer there is sunlight almost all day and all night. It's difficult to live without sunlight. But it isn't easy with too much light, either. It's hard to sleep when the sun is shining all night!

[11] **allergic:** when you get sick if you eat or touch certain things

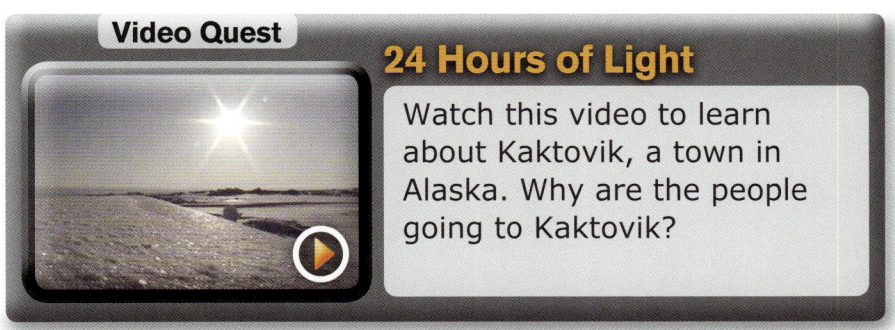

Video Quest

24 Hours of Light

Watch this video to learn about Kaktovik, a town in Alaska. Why are the people going to Kaktovik?

A volcano erupts with lava and gases.

The sun is our main **source** of natural light. However, there are other natural light sources on the Earth. Lava and gases that erupt from volcanoes make light. Even if there isn't any sunlight, people can see lava and these gases in the dark.

Light is made during an earthquake, too. For years, people said they saw light from earthquakes. Finally, photographs taken in the 1960s during an earthquake in Japan showed this light. Earthquake light is usually white, red, or blue. People aren't sure exactly why earthquakes make this light. Some scientists think that maybe rocks in the earth have energy that comes out during an earthquake.

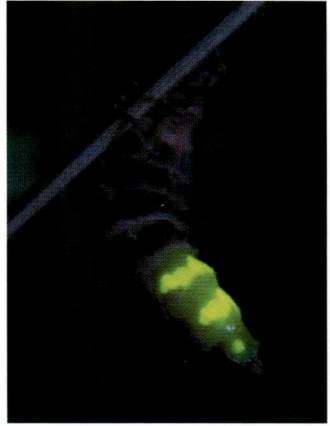

A glowworm   A firefly

Some animals make their own light. Fireflies and glowworms make light to protect[12] themselves. Glowworms make light to scare other animals, and some fireflies make light to show they aren't good to eat.

The alarm jellyfish makes light to protect itself, too. When a fish tries to eat the alarm jellyfish, the jellyfish turns on its light. The jellyfish wants a bigger fish to see the light and attack the smaller fish. When this happens, the jellyfish swims away.

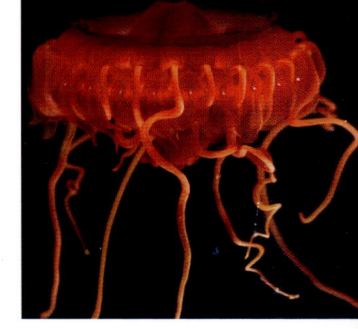

An alarm jellyfish

In Vieques, Puerto Rico, there is a body of water with many small organisms[13] that make light. At night, the water shines bright blue. The light is so bright that you can read a book by the water!

[12] **protect:** keep safe from something dangerous or bad
[13] **organism:** a living thing, often a very small one

CHAPTER 4

Artificial Light

HOW HAVE PEOPLE MADE LIGHT?

People used candles for light at night until the light bulb was invented.

Think about how you use artificial light every day. In the morning, a light on your alarm clock shows the time. When you use your computer, television, and phone, their screens light up. Traffic lights tell you when to stop and go when you drive. You turn on lights in your car and in your house at night. These are just some of the ways you use artificial light. Now think about living without artificial light. How different would your life be?

In the past, people used fire for light at night. Then from 3,000 BCE, people started using candles. After that lamps were invented.[14] People used oil and gas to light the lamps. Finally, in 1879, Thomas Edison invented a safe and easy way to use the electric light bulb. His invention changed our world.

[14]**invent:** make something new

Before the light bulb, people did not do much at night because it was dark. Electric light changed that. Businesses grew. People could do more at night, and they could do things during the day more easily. If you look at a picture of our planet from space at night, you can see how the light bulb changed life on Earth.

North America with lights shining from Earth.

We depend on[15] electric light from energy sources like oil, gas, or coal. But those energy sources create pollution. One answer to this problem is to use a cleaner source of energy, for example **solar power**. Scientists have found a way to capture[16] the energy of the sun's light and save it to use later. So now the sun can light our homes at night!

[15]**depend on:** need the help of someone or something
[16]**capture:** catch something

This home uses solar power for heat and light.

Another form of artificial light is **laser** light. Remember that light from the sun has seven colors. So does light from a light bulb. Each laser light, however, has only one color. But different laser lights have different colors. The most usual color is red. Laser light does not spread out like natural light or light from a light bulb. It travels in a thin straight line.

Laser light was first used successfully in 1960, but it didn't become popular for many years. Today, laser light is used for many things. Lasers are used at music concerts to create beautiful light shows. They are also used in hospitals, for example, to repair some eye problems. And lasers are used in industry[17] to cut wood or metal.

[17] **industry:** all the companies that make things

A laser light show at a concert

After people found out how to make artificial light, they found many interesting ways to use it. Dentists, for example, use special lights to make our teeth whiter. And farmers use artificial light to grow plants indoors all year round. This is useful in places where it gets cold in the winter.

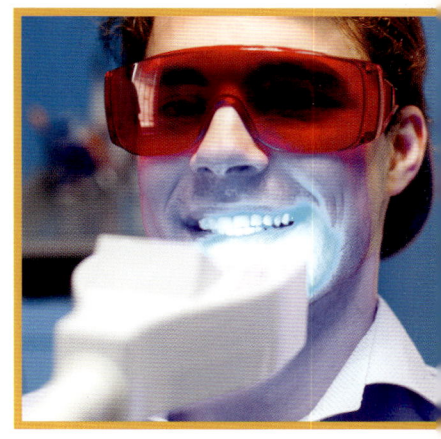

People often get depressed[18] when they don't get much sunlight. So in places where it is dark all year, people use special lights called daylight lamps in their homes. The light from these lamps is similar to the sun's light, and people say it makes them feel better.

[18] **depressed:** very sad, often for a long time

People don't only use light for things they need or want. People use light to make art. They use light in plays, movies, and TV shows. For example, light can make it look like daytime at night.

Before the invention of the light bulb, you had to watch plays during the day when it was light outside. Now we usually go to the theatre in the evening.

Light can also be used to change the way we feel. Think of a scene[19] in a movie. It's dark. The moonlight shines through the window. You feel afraid. Suddenly, someone switches on the light, and you don't feel afraid any more.

[19]**scene:** a short part of a movie or play in which things happen in one place

Video Quest

Lighting Designer

Watch this video to learn about a **lighting designer's** job. What are some things a lighting designer does?

Light goes through a hole in a camera.

Cameras can't work without light. A camera has a hole in it that opens and closes. When you take a picture of something, light reflects off it. This reflected light enters the camera through the hole. The light then hits the film[20] or a computer chip[21] to make a picture. The hole can open and close quickly or stay open for a few seconds. When it opens very wide, it lets in a lot of light. When it opens a little, it doesn't let in much light.

There is even something called light art. Artists use artificial light to create art. Chul Hyun Ahn is a light artist from Korea. Some of his light art has been in museums around the world.

[20]**film:** a special thin plastic used for making photographs
[21]**chip:** a very small part of a computer that stores information

CHAPTER 5

What Do You Think?

IS IT BETTER TO LIVE IN THE LIGHT OR IN THE DARK?

In places that are very far north, it is dark most of the time in the winter and light in the summer. Amy lives in Fairbanks, Alaska. Read about her life "in the dark" and "in the light."

"In the winter, it is very dark here. This is called the polar night. Some people think the sun never shines, but we do get a little sunlight. We usually don't see the sun in the sky, but there is a little light in the sky for a few hours each day. The rest of the time, it is dark. It can be difficult. People get depressed when they don't get enough sun. I have special lamps in my home. They are very bright, and they really help.

Sometimes, I go to see the Northern Lights in the winter. These happen during certain times of the year when gas from the sun enters the Earth's atmosphere.[22] It makes red, green, blue, and violet lights in the night sky. It's one of the most beautiful things I've ever seen!

[22]**atmosphere:** the gases around Earth

In the summer, it is light all day and night. This is called the polar day. We also call it "the midnight sun," because it is sunny even at midnight. I often go for boat rides at night with my friends. One time, we had a picnic at midnight! In June, there is a race called the Midnight Sun Run. People come from all over Alaska to run in the race. It starts at 10:00 p.m. Every year, on July 4th, there is a baseball game at midnight. It's fun to have so much sunlight, but it can also be difficult. I'm tired after a busy day, and it's hard to sleep. I have very dark curtains on my windows to block out the sun, and they help."

1. You are planning a trip to Fairbanks, Alaska. Do you want to go in the summer or in the winter? Why? Write your opinion or discuss in groups.

2. Think about living in Fairbanks. What will you do you when it is dark most of the day? How will you feel? What will you do when it is light all the time? How will you feel?

Midnight Sun Run, Alaska, 10:00 p.m.

After You Read

Read the following sentences and choose Ⓐ, Ⓑ, or Ⓒ.

1 Expressions with "light" are often about things _____.
- Ⓐ getting worse
- Ⓑ getting better
- Ⓒ expanding

2 The Moon gets its light from the _____.
- Ⓐ sun
- Ⓑ stars
- Ⓒ Earth

3 When two stars hit each other in a star cluster, they become _____.
- Ⓐ a new cluster
- Ⓑ one bright star
- Ⓒ two smaller stars

Video

4 A light year is how far light _____ in one year.
- Ⓐ turns
- Ⓑ reflects
- Ⓒ travels

5 Too much sun can give someone _____.
- Ⓐ a sunburn or a rash
- Ⓑ too much energy
- Ⓒ problems with blood

6 _____ have natural light.
- Ⓐ The moon and planets
- Ⓑ Fireflies and alarm jellyfish
- Ⓒ Lamps and light bulbs

7 People can use _____ to get energy for lights in their homes.
- Ⓐ moonlight
- Ⓑ laser lights
- Ⓒ solar power

Complete the Text

Use the words in the box to complete the paragraph.

cosmologist   energy   planets   spread   universe

Our Expanding World
Tuesdays at 7:00 p.m.

Our **❶** _____ started small, but it
❷ _____ out over time. Watch "Our Expanding
World" to learn about space and time. **❸** _____
Dr. Bryan Sumner shows us how things work in space. You'll learn about
❹ _____ from the sun. You'll learn a lot about
Earth and the other **❺** _____. Don't miss this
show if you want to understand more about our world.

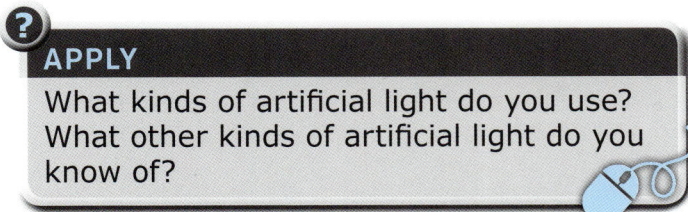

?

APPLY

What kinds of artificial light do you use?
What other kinds of artificial light do you
know of?

Answer Key

Words to Know, page 4
① Planets ② Cosmologists ③ universe ④ energy

Apply, page 4
Answers will vary.

Words to Know, page 5
① shines ② reflects ③ Artificial light ④ lasers ⑤ wave

Understand, page 7
Answers will vary.

Video Quest, page 11
Proxima Centauri is 4.2 light years away, and Sirius is 8½ light years away.

Video Quest, page 15
The people are going to Kaktovik to study how animals live in that area.

Video Quest, page 22
A lighting designer decides all the different types of lights that are going to be used, what colors they're going to be, where they're going to be hung, and when they're going to be turned on and off during the show.

Choose the Correct Answers, page 26
① b ② a ③ b ④ c ⑤ a ⑥ b ⑦ c

Complete the Text, page 27
① universe ② spread ③ Cosmologist ④ energy
⑤ planets

Apply, page 27
Answers will vary.